GUARDIANS OF THE GALAXY

A GUIDE TO THE COSMIC ADVENTURERS

BY MARC SUMERAK

A Division of Insight Editions, LP

San Rafael, California

MARVEL

GUARDIANS OF THE GALAXY

A GUIDE TO THE COSMIC ADVENTURERS

BY MARC SUMERAK

INCREDI BUILDS™

A Division of Insight Editions, LP
San Rafael, California

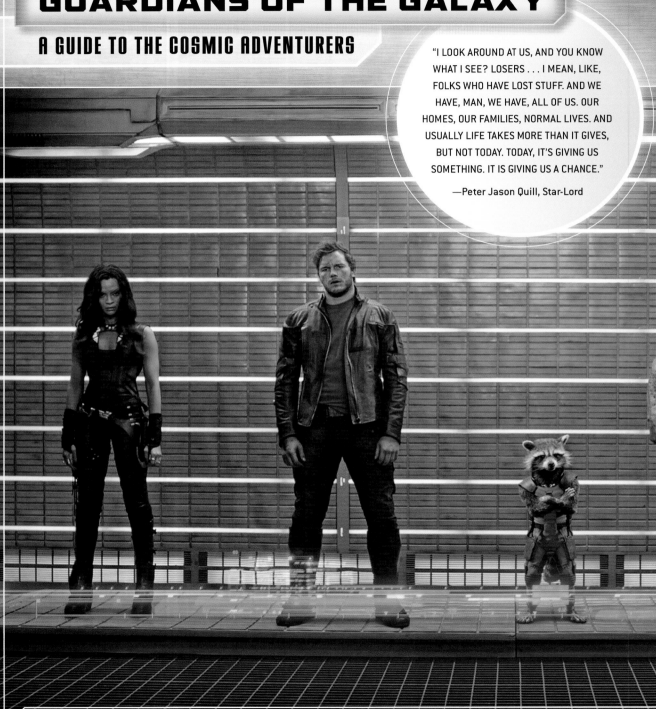

GUARDIANS OF THE GALAXY

A GUIDE TO THE COSMIC ADVENTURERS

"I LOOK AROUND AT US, AND YOU KNOW WHAT I SEE? LOSERS . . . I MEAN, LIKE, FOLKS WHO HAVE LOST STUFF. AND WE HAVE, MAN, WE HAVE, ALL OF US. OUR HOMES, OUR FAMILIES, NORMAL LIVES. AND USUALLY LIFE TAKES MORE THAN IT GIVES, BUT NOT TODAY. TODAY, IT'S GIVING US SOMETHING. IT IS GIVING US A CHANCE."

—Peter Jason Quill, Star-Lord

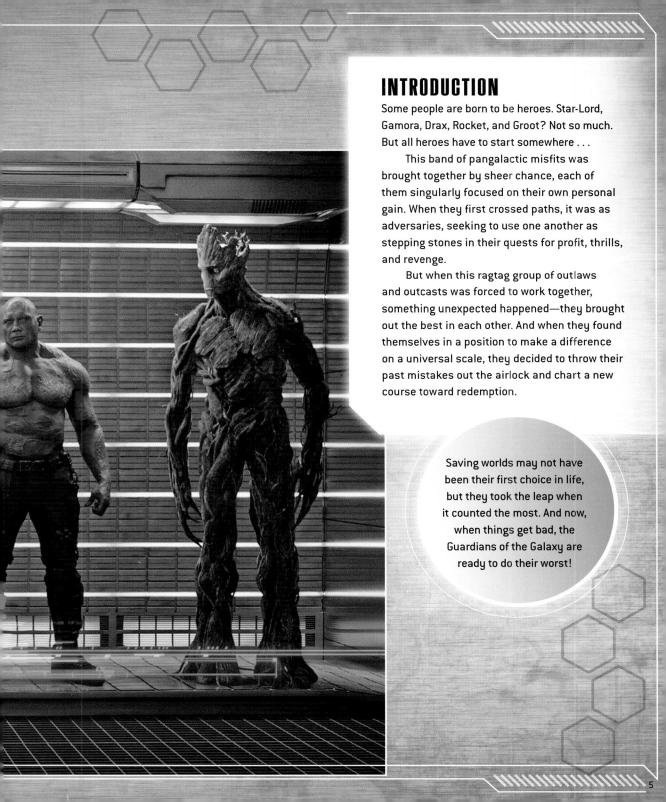

INTRODUCTION

Some people are born to be heroes. Star-Lord, Gamora, Drax, Rocket, and Groot? Not so much. But all heroes have to start somewhere . . .

This band of pangalactic misfits was brought together by sheer chance, each of them singularly focused on their own personal gain. When they first crossed paths, it was as adversaries, seeking to use one another as stepping stones in their quests for profit, thrills, and revenge.

But when this ragtag group of outlaws and outcasts was forced to work together, something unexpected happened—they brought out the best in each other. And when they found themselves in a position to make a difference on a universal scale, they decided to throw their past mistakes out the airlock and chart a new course toward redemption.

Saving worlds may not have been their first choice in life, but they took the leap when it counted the most. And now, when things get bad, the Guardians of the Galaxy are ready to do their worst!

STAR-LORD

Born on Earth but drawn to the stars, Peter Quill became the interstellar adventurer known as Star-Lord. Quill acquires an immensely powerful artifact and attracts the attention of those who would use its power to spread the chaos and destruction. Equipped with high-tech weaponry, a dependable starship, and a mixtape of music from home, the headstrong Star-Lord must rally an unlikely team of misfits—the Guardians of the Galaxy—for an all-or-nothing attempt to protect the cosmos.

AWESOME MIX

Peter and his mother shared a love of Terran pop culture, including classic rock music. A cassette tape made by his mother featuring a collection of her favorite songs, dubbed *Awesome Mix Vol. 1*, helped Peter through one of the toughest times in his life: his mother's untimely death. On her deathbed, Peter's mother gave her son a present. Peter would wait years before finally coming to terms with his loss and opening the box, revealing the long-awaited *Awesome Mix Vol. 2*.

OUT OF THIS WORLD

Immediately after his mother passed away, a grief-stricken young Peter ran from the hospital. He could never have anticipated what awaited him outside—an alien ship that beamed him on board. What could have been a terrifying turn of events instead ended up being just the escape that the distraught boy needed.

Peter spent the next twenty-six years of his life as part of a crew of spacefaring mercenaries known as the Ravagers, shaping himself into a swashbuckling space pirate worthy of the name given to him by his mother. He became Star-Lord . . . and the galaxy would never be the same!

ALL DRESSED UP

Star-Lord's red leather jacket may be easily recognizable as the trademark garb of the Ravagers, but he doesn't let the look define him. Star-Lord carries a number of his own high-tech accessories with him on missions, including a translator implant, a quad blaster, boot jets, and a retractable helmet with integrated scanning, communication, and life support systems. He also carries one extremely low-tech item with him: an archaic Terran cassette player loaded with the aforementioned *Awesome Mix*.

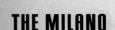

THE MILANO

Star-Lord's personal starship, a Ravager M-ship dubbed the *Milano*, is more than just a sweet ride—it's his home. Decked out with all of his remaining Terran memorabilia, including vintage stereo equipment, the *Milano* is the perfect balance of Star-Lord's past and present. After the *Milano* was destroyed during a battle against Ronan the Accuser, the ship was rebuilt by the Nova Corps using parts salvaged from the original.

THE RAVAGERS

Star-Lord eventually came to view the Ravagers as his dysfunctional family, but their relationship didn't exactly start out on the right foot. In fact, he came close to being eaten by members of the crew on more than one occasion, simply because they hadn't tasted a Terran before.

The Ravagers originally abducted young Peter Quill from Terra as part of a job. Quill's mysterious father had hired the Ravagers to locate and return the boy to him after the death of his mother. When the Ravagers' captain, Yondu Udonta, developed a fondness for the young Terran, he decided to abandon the mission and keep Quill on board as a member of the crew. The Ravagers live by one code only: steal everything from everybody. That is, of course, unless you're stealing from another Ravager. Then things can get ugly . . . fast!

YONDU UDONTA

The no-nonsense captain of the Ravagers, Yondu Udonta is always ready to lead his band of thieves and pirates into battle . . . as long as there's something in it for him. Yondu is a strong, charismatic leader, able to keep even the most unruly members of his crew in line. He has also proven to be an expert pilot and combatant. Yondu's signature weapon, the yaka arrow—a metal projectile that can be controlled through a series of high-pitched whistles—has skewered uncountable foes.

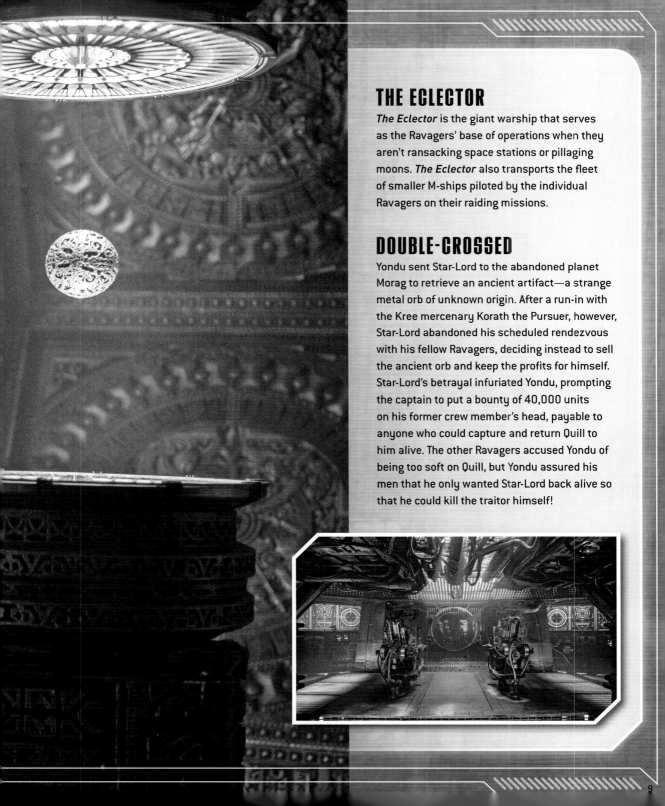

THE ECLECTOR

The Eclector is the giant warship that serves as the Ravagers' base of operations when they aren't ransacking space stations or pillaging moons. *The Eclector* also transports the fleet of smaller M-ships piloted by the individual Ravagers on their raiding missions.

DOUBLE-CROSSED

Yondu sent Star-Lord to the abandoned planet Morag to retrieve an ancient artifact—a strange metal orb of unknown origin. After a run-in with the Kree mercenary Korath the Pursuer, however, Star-Lord abandoned his scheduled rendezvous with his fellow Ravagers, deciding instead to sell the ancient orb and keep the profits for himself. Star-Lord's betrayal infuriated Yondu, prompting the captain to put a bounty of 40,000 units on his former crew member's head, payable to anyone who could capture and return Quill to him alive. The other Ravagers accused Yondu of being too soft on Quill, but Yondu assured his men that he only wanted Star-Lord back alive so that he could kill the traitor himself!

KORATH THE PURSUER

Star-Lord and the Ravagers were not the only ones hoping to recover the mysterious Orb. Moments after the artifact was in Star-Lord's hands, he found himself confronted by the cybernetically enhanced Kree mercenary known as Korath the Pursuer. Korath sought to retrieve the Orb for his master, Ronan, and was not about to let some paltry thief walk away with it. Not seeing Star-Lord as a threat, Korath attempted to take the outlaw as his prisoner. However, Star-Lord managed to escape with the Orb, leaving Korath to return to Ronan empty-handed. Though he may not have been able to retrieve the Orb, Korath was able to determine the ultimate destination of its new owner—Xandar.

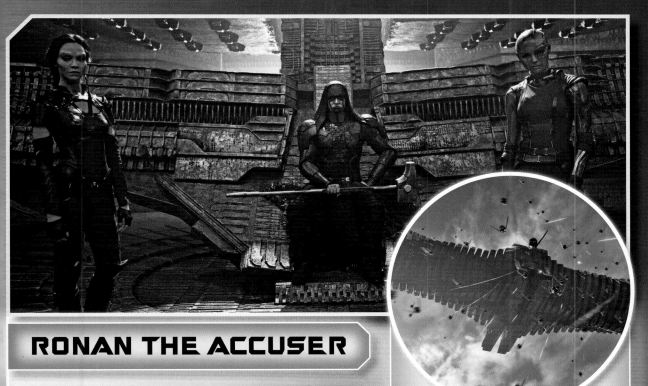

RONAN THE ACCUSER

The being known as Ronan commands a massive fleet of Necrocraft from his warship, the Dark Aster. Strength is all that matters to Ronan—he sees all weakness as a disease, an unforgivable crime of which the entire galaxy stands accused. Wielding his menacing Cosmi-Rod, Ronan seeks to cure this sickness by bringing about total chaos and has laid waste to many worlds in pursuit of a powerful artifact that will help him achieve this goal.

In order to foster the total annihilation of Xandarian culture, Ronan made a pact with an extraterrestrial warlord named Thanos. Ronan promised to locate the Orb for Thanos in exchange for the complete destruction Xandar—a simple deal that Star-Lord managed to unwittingly complicate.

Unwilling to accept any further failure, Ronan dispatched one of Thanos's own daughters, Gamora, to intercept Star-Lord on Xandar and retrieve the Orb.

THE DARK ASTER

Ronan's warship, the *Dark Aster*, was a flying fortress housing Ronan, his Kree followers, and hundreds of Sakaaran soldiers. *The Dark Aster* was eventually destroyed during the Battle of Xandar.

THE SAKAARANS

The insect-like Sakaarans are common allies of the Kree and often aid them in military endeavors.Ronan and Korath employed the services of hundreds of these soldiers during their campaign against Xandar. Though formidable combatants and pilots, the Sakaarans tend to be perceived by their foes as a nothing more than cannon fodder.

GAMORA

The last surviving member of her species, Gamora was transformed into an unparalleled warrior through rigorous training and physiological augmentation. For years, Gamora has used her formidable fighting skills and master swordsmanship in service to a dark power, earning her the reputation of the "most dangerous woman in the universe." Gamora now seeks redemption for her past crimes as a member of the Guardians of the Galaxy, and waits for an opportunity to bring vengeance to those who have manipulated her.

Thanos lent the services of Gamora and her adopted sister, Nebula, to Ronan during his quest for the Orb and his attacks on Xandar. Though Gamora served her masters with unwavering loyalty at first, she could not bear to watch her adopted father destroy another planet. She secretly put her own plans into motion to remove the Orb from play and ensure that Ronan's deal with Thanos would not come to pass.

NEBULA

Another of Thanos's daughters, Nebula was a cold and calculated killer who constantly found herself in Gamora's shadow. Like her sister, Nebula's body was augmented with a number of cybernetic enhancements, including a powerful robotic arm. Although seemingly loyal to her father's megalomaniacal whims, Nebula deeply resented the horrific transformation that Thanos forced upon her.

When Gamora decided to go rogue and betray Ronan, Nebula was more than glad to confront her sister in combat. After multiple encounters, Nebula was eventually bested by Gamora. Rather than suffer her estranged sister's newfound heroic whims, Nebula instead severed her own mechanical hand to ensure her escape.

THANOS

The Mad Titan known as Thanos is one of the most powerful beings in the universe. An intergalactic conqueror, Thanos has amassed great armies and obliterated entire planets. His desire for ultimate power has led him to seek out a number of ancient cosmic artifacts, including the Tesseract and the Orb.

Thanos rarely bothers to get his own hands dirty, instead having others carry out his bidding for him. But should he feel dissatisfied or betrayed by his allies, the Mad Titan is not afraid to bathe the starways in their blood.

Thanos holds court in the deep-space realm known as Sanctuary. There, he rules from his floating throne, plotting the next twisted step on his path toward complete universal domination.

THE OTHER

The being known only as The Other served as a primary liaison between Thanos and those bold enough to do business with him. The Other helped orchestrate many of Thanos's attempts to acquire objects of power. As an intermediary, The Other often incurred the wrath intended for Thanos, including a violent outburst from Ronan, who snapped his neck and ended his life.

WELCOME TO XANDAR

Xandar is the capital world of the Nova Empire. A generally peaceful and prosperous civilization, the Xandarians take pride in their diverse population and technological advancements. After a thousand years of fighting against the Kree, the Xandarian government finally managed to broker a peace treaty between the warring empires. With extremists such as Ronan eager to fracture the fragile accords, though, the people of Xandar looked to their elite military forces for protection.

THE NOVA CORPS

Xandar is the home base of one of the largest assemblages of peacekeepers in the universe: the Nova Corps. These no-nonsense lawmen patrol the planet—and the universe—making sure that anyone who breaks the rules is brought to justice. If you commit a crime on Xandar, the Nova Corps will find you.

The Nova Corps also mans a number of prisons and outposts throughout the universe, many of which were attacked and destroyed by Ronan and his followers during their rebellion against the Xandarian peace treaty.

The uniform of the Nova Corps features a glowing tri-star design inspired by the three suns that light Xandar's skies.

NOVA PRIME

The leader of the Nova Corps, Nova Prime Irani Rael, was instrumental in constructing the peace treaty with the Kree Empire. When Ronan began assaulting Nova outposts as a precursor to his attack on Xandar, Nova Prime contacted the Kree government to intervene. The Kree refused to condemn Ronan's actions, leaving Xandar and the Nova Corps to fend for themselves. A commanding presence, Nova Prime led her forces through some of Xandar's darkest hours and managed to emerge triumphant.

RHOMANN DEY

Nova Corpsman Rhomann Dey may not openly admit it, but he is actually kind of fond of Peter Quill—whom he mockingly identified as "Star-Prince" during their early encounters. Despite the strict laws of the Nova Corps, Dey proved himself willing to trust those attempting to protect his people—even outlaws like Star-Lord. His instincts helped give Xandar the chance to prepare for Ronan's coming onslaught. Dey was promoted to the Denarian rank after the Battle of Xandar.

GARTHAN SAAL

Completely by the books, Denarian Garthan Saal did not tolerate criminals and hoodlums on his planet. Yet when Xandar was in peril, he put aside his distaste for those outlaws and joined them in the fight against Ronan's forces. Saal helped initiate a blockade made up of hundreds of Nova ships in order to slow the *Dark Aster*'s descent towards Xandar, a maneuver that cost him his life but may have saved the planet he had sworn to protect.

STAR BLASTERS

The personal craft of the Nova Corps, Star Blasters possess a number of offensive and defensive capabilities crucial in keeping the peace on Xandar and beyond. These small one-man ships are fitted with offensive laser cannons, tractor beams for detaining criminals, and a unique energy field that allows multiple Star Blasters to link together and create a blockade.

THE BROKER

DESPITE THE LOOMING NOVA CORPS PRESENCE on Xandar, Star-Lord visited the planet in hopes of selling the Orb to a dealer of rare, high-end antiques known as The Broker. Once The Broker learned that Ronan was after the Orb, however, he broke off negotiations with Star-Lord and forced the outlaw to leave his shop immediately.

MEET-SHOOT

After Star-Lord was ejected from The Broker's shop, he encountered someone else willing to take the Orb off his hands: Gamora. Swiping the relic from Star-Lord, Gamora initiated a wild chase through the populated Xandarian streets. The Orb exchanged hands several times as Star-Lord and Gamora attempted to outrun, outwit, and outfight each other. Neither of them had anticipated how formidable their opponent would be . . . and they certainly couldn't have foreseen the arrival of the galaxy's most unusual pair of bounty hunters.

ROCKET

Despite his diminutive stature and raccoon-like appearance, the scrappy mercenary known as Rocket possesses a remarkable mastery of munitions and battle tactics. A host of illegal genetic and cybernetic experiments on the planet Half-World have ensured that Rocket is the only creature of his type in all the cosmos, and until recently he has been content to roam the stars in search of adventure and fast cash with his partner in crime, Groot. But when an ominous threat leaves the entire universe at risk, Rocket must bring his mechanical genius and ingenuity to bear as a member of the Guardians of the Galaxy.

GROOT

The tree-like Groot hails from a mysterious world designated only as "X." The taciturn Groot makes up for his limited vocabulary with his ability to grow and manipulate his giant, bark-covered form as needed—skills he has long used to aid and abet his friend Rocket Raccoon's schemes. Now as the fate of the cosmos hangs in the balance, Groot must join the Guardians of the Galaxy for an adventure that will test the limits of even his monstrous strength.

ALL OR NOTHING

While the duo was looking for their next big score on Xandar, Rocket's scanners locked onto Star-Lord and identified the bounty placed on him by Yondu. Unwilling to pass on a 40,000-unit payday, Rocket and Groot attempted to ambush the rogue Ravager, only to end up getting caught up in Star-Lord's deadly dance with Gamora. The furious fight that followed caught the attention of the local authorities, and instead of cashing in their paychecks, Rocket and Groot found themselves in Nova Corps custody, heading to a deep-space prison alongside Star-Lord and Gamora.

THE KYLN

After being processed by Nova Corpsmen Dey and Saal, the quartet of newly captured criminals was transported to the Kyln—a deep-space maximum security prison for the universe's nastiest offenders. Although Star-Lord and his new companions seemingly had little in common with each other, Rocket and Groot decided to protect Quill from the Kyln's violent general population . . . at least until they could collect the bounty on him later.

The Kyln's residents were more interested in one of the other new arrivals, however, as Gamora quickly learned how universally hated she was for the cruelties she had committed while serving under Thanos and Ronan. When some of the Kyln's more unsavory occupants attempted to abduct and kill her, they were interrupted by another inmate who felt that he alone had earned the right to end her murderous ways once and for all.

DRAX THE DESTROYER

Fueled by a personal vendetta against those that cost him his family, the rough-edged warrior called Drax the Destroyer has room in his life for little else besides revenge. At Thanos's behest, Ronan had slaughtered Drax's wife and daughter. In turn, Drax massacred dozens of Ronan's minions in his quest for revenge before eventually ending up incarcerated in the Kyln. Upon Gamora's arrival, Drax saw the opportunity to kill a member of Thanos's "family" as payback for the death of his own.

Before Gamora and Drax were able to harm each other, Star-Lord jumped in, suggesting that Gamora might be of more value alive. After all, since she had betrayed Ronan, the Kree warlord was likely to come looking for her. That could potentially lead Drax directly to the man he actually wanted to kill. With a momentary truce called, Star-Lord and his new companions focused their attention on a far more important challenge: escaping the Kyln.

PRISON BREAK

Busting out of a high-security Nova Corps detention facility is no easy task . . . but for Rocket, who had already managed to escape incarceration twenty-two times previously, it seemed like just another day on the job.

Rocket devised an elaborate plan with Star-Lord and Gamora that involved stealing a quarnyx battery, a Nova guardsman's security band, and a prisoner's prosthetic limb. Unfortunately, things went horribly wrong when an eager Groot put his part of the plan into action much earlier than anticipated. Chaos erupted, but, with help from Drax, the band of misfits still managed to break into the prison's main control tower and orchestrate a daring escape.

Before departing the Kyln, the group reclaimed their confiscated personal items—including Star-Lord's cassette player, the Orb, and Star-Lord's ship, the *Milano*. For their assistance, Gamora offered her new allies an equal share of the profits from the Orb's impending sale—a whopping four billion units!

GOING KNOWHERE

On the edge of the universe floats Knowhere, a mining colony built inside the severed cranium of a giant Celestial being. Hundreds of years ago, the Tivan Group laid claim to the enormous decapitated head and began to mine the rare organic matter found within it. The Celestial's bone, brain tissue, and spinal fluid became highly valued in black markets across the galaxy. The mining operations at Knowhere were a dangerous and illegal line of work, suitable only for outlaws. Because of this, Knowhere became the perfect hideaway for the galaxy's most wanted criminals to drink, gamble, and indulge their darkest curiosities.

Star-Lord and his new companions arrived on Knowhere and ventured into a less-than-respectable drinking establishment, the Boot of Jemiah, as they waited for Gamora's buyer to contact them. During this rare, quiet moment, Star-Lord and Gamora began to connect on a more personal level. Rocket and Drax, on the other hand, became highly intoxicated and nearly murdered each other. Star-Lord diffused the situation, but an enraged Drax stormed away from the group just as the buyer's envoy, Carina, came to fetch them.

THE COLLECTOR

Taneleer Tivan, also known as The Collector, maintained the galaxy's largest assortment of fauna, relics, and species of all manners. This eccentric being was the head of the Tivan Group and had used his fortune to populate an enormous museum with the universe's most unusual and powerful creatures and objects—from Dark Elves and Chitauri to telepathic dogs and talking ducks.

For The Collector, adding to his assortment of artifacts had become an obsession. The more unique the item, the more he was willing to pay. And there was no price too high for what was contained inside the Orb—an Infinity Stone.

INFINITY STONES

Before all of creation, there were six singularities. When the universe exploded into existence, the remnants of those systems were forged into the concentrated ingots of unimaginable power known as the Infinity Stones and scattered across reality.

Infinity Stones can only be wielded by beings of extraordinary strength. Long ago, the god-like Celestials used the stones to destroy entire civilizations. Once, a group of powerful beings was able to share the raw energy of the Infinity Stones amongst themselves, but they were quickly destroyed by it.

Three of the six Infinity Stones were recently identified: the Tesseract, the Scepter, and the Aether. The Aether was already in The Collector's possession, but he desired the full set. He believed that the Orb of Morag housed a fourth Infinity Stone. When the Orb opened to reveal the glowing purple gem inside, The Collector's suspicions were justified.

CARINA'S BETRAYAL

Before The Collector could pay Gamora and her companions for their delivery of the Infinity Stone, his servant, Carina, grabbed ahold of the glowing gem in a desperate attempt to break free of The Collector's enslavement. Instead, the Infinity Stone disintegrated her body and released an intense burst of energy that nearly obliterated The Collector's menagerie. Star-Lord, Gamora, Rocket, and Groot narrowly escaped with their lives.

HERE COMES TROUBLE

Star-Lord and Gamora managed to recover the Orb—and the Infinity Stone contained within it—during the explosion of The Collector's gallery. But their problems were far from over. While they had been inside negotiating with The Collector, a vengeful Drax had placed a call to Ronan, luring the Kree warlord to Knowhere with information on the whereabouts of Gamora and the Orb. Drax saw this as an opportunity to finally come face-to-face with his greatest foe and destroy him. As if a fleet of Kree radicals weren't enough of a problem, Yondu and the Ravagers had also tracked Star-Lord to Knowhere, arriving at almost the exact same moment as Ronan.

RAVAGED

Star-Lord, Rocket, and Gamora hijacked Tivan Group mining pods and found themselves in a dogfight with a squadron of Sakaaran Necrocraft. One of the Necrocraft, piloted by Nebula, destroyed Gamora's mining pod outside of Knowhere's artificial atmosphere. Gamora almost died in the void of space before Star-Lord rescued her, nearly sacrificing his own life in the process. To survive, Star-Lord had to broadcast his coordinates to the Ravagers, surrendering himself to the former allies he had betrayed. Star-Lord and Gamora were beamed safely aboard the *Eclector*, with only moments to spare.

DESTROYER DESTROYED

Back on the ground, Drax was handily beaten by his archnemesis, Ronan, and left for dead. Ronan took his leave from Knowhere with the Orb in his possession. After being revived by Groot, a humiliated Drax realized that he had let anger cloud his judgement and that his new friends had paid the price. Groot and Drax decided to band together in an attempt to rescue Star-Lord and Gamora from the Ravagers, despite Rocket's initial misgivings.

ROCKET TO THE RESCUE

Rocket came around and cobbled together a powerful weapon that he called a Hadron Enforcer, which he threatened to use to blow up the *Eclector* if his friends weren't safely returned. Luckily, Star-Lord and Gamora had already convinced Yondu and the Ravagers to keep them alive by offering to help them steal back the Orb from Ronan. Star-Lord promised the Orb—and any profits made from its sale—to Yondu in exchange for their lives.

With the Ravagers now on their side, Star-Lord was convinced that he and his companions could stop Ronan from destroying Xandar. After all, he had a plan. Well, at least part of a plan . . .

TWELVE PERCENT OF A PLAN

Because the Infinity Stone reacted to anything organic, all Ronan had to do was touch the stone to Xandar's surface and all of the plants, animals, and people on the planet would die. So the most important step of Star-Lord's plan was to make sure that Ronan never made it to the ground with the Orb.

To achieve this, Rocket would lead a team of Ravager M-ships to blow a hole in the *Dark Aster*'s starboard hull. Then Star-Lord and his crew would enter the *Dark Aster* via that opening. Once aware of the breach, Ronan would likely seal himself behind impenetrable security doors. Luckily Gamora knew where the controls for those doors were located and would be able to dismantle their power source. When the team arrived on the flight deck, they would be able to kill Ronan using the Hadron Enforcer. They would then retrieve the Infinity Stone using a newly designed containment Orb and, as promised, deliver it to Yondu.

ASSAULT ON XANDAR

The only reliable thing about plans is that they never go according to plan.

Rocket was able to blast an entry point into the *Dark Aster*'s hull for his teammates, and Star-Lord's crew was able to get inside and defeat Korath, Nebula, and dozens of Sakaaran soldiers in combat. But they never anticipated that Ronan had already opened the Orb and integrated the Infinity Stone into his hammer! With the Stone's power at his command, Ronan was able to survive the blast from the Hadron Enforcer and turn his wrath against his new enemies.

Meanwhile, Rocket and the Ravagers had another unexpected problem as Ronan ordered his fleet of Sakaaran Necrocraft to crash their ships directly into Xandar's surface, sacrificing his forces to create as much chaos and damage as possible.

THE CAVALRY

Luckily, Star-Lord had already placed a call to Rhomann Dey—the same Nova Corps officer who had arrested him earlier—warning him of the impending danger to Xandar. Dey presented the information to Nova Prime and, despite its unreliable source, insisted that the threat was indeed real. This gave the Nova Corps time to evacuate the city and join the fight before things got too far out of control. Garthan Saal led hundreds of Nova Corps Star Blasters in the creation of a blockade to slow down the *Dark Aster*'s descent.

FALL OF THE DARK ASTER

Ronan used the power of the Infinity Stone to annihilate the Nova Corps blockade, destroying the ships and killing their pilots. Rocket realized that the only way to take down Ronan was to follow the Sakaarans' lead and steer his ship straight into the *Dark Aster*'s main flight deck. Rocket's last minute plan worked, sending the *Dark Aster* plummeting towards Xandar—with Star-Lord, Gamora, Drax, Rocket, and Groot inside!

WE ARE GROOT

As the *Dark Aster* plummeted towards Xandar, Groot extended his limbs and vines, creating a protective sphere around his new friends. This proved enough to save them from harm during the ship's impact. However, in the process of saving his new friends, Groot's wooden body was reduced to splinters.

DANCE-OFF!

Ronan survived the crash as well. Before he could use the Infinity Stone on Xandar, however, he was challenged to an unexpected form of combat by Star-Lord—a dance-off! Caught off guard by Star-Lord's bizarre antics, Ronan was distracted long enough for Drax and Rocket to fire the Hadron Enforcer once again—this time targeting Ronan's hammer. As the Universal Weapon shattered, the Infinity Stone was launched into the air.

POWER GRAB

Star-Lord instinctively leaped to grab the Infinity Stone, which almost immediately began to dissolve his physical form with its overwhelming power. Gamora, Drax, and Rocket all grabbed onto Star-Lord, using their bodies to help channel the gem's intense energy. Together, they redirected the Infinity Stone's power to wipe Ronan from existence.

GALAXY = GUARDED

Immediately after Ronan's defeat, Gamora enclosed the Infinity Stone safely inside a new Orb. Yondu arrived to claim the Orb, as agreed upon previously. Star-Lord handed it over, begging Yondu never to open it due to the dangerous power it contained. As the Ravagers departed, Star-Lord revealed that he had swapped Orbs at the last second. Yondu had actually departed with a decoy, and the real Orb with the Infinity Stone inside was still in Star-Lord's possession.

Star-Lord and his team, now calling themselves the Guardians of the Galaxy, handed over the Infinity Stone to the Nova Corps for safekeeping. In exchange for their bravery, they received full pardons for all of their past crimes. Additionally, the Nova Corps rebuilt the *Milano*, which had been destroyed during the battle against the *Dark Aster*, as a sign of their gratitude.

Star-Lord also learned that his mother had been correct all those years ago. His father actually was from space, and Quill's hybrid physiology was unlike any the Nova Corps had seen before. In fact, it had likely been his alien genetics that had allowed him to survive contact with the Infinity Stone for as long as he did.

As Star-Lord and his new crew took to the skies again, it looked like they were ready for a fresh start. Even Groot was beginning to regenerate via a twig salvaged from the *Dark Aster*'s wreckage. Now, with a new cassette in the stereo and unlimited possibilities ahead, the Guardians of the Galaxy had only one decision left to make about what to do next:

"Something good? Something bad? Bit of both?"

"Bit of both."

MAKE IT YOUR OWN

One of the great things about IncrediBuilds models is that each one is completely customizable. The untreated natural wood can be decorated with paints, pencils, pens, beads, sequins—the list goes on and on!

Before you start building and decorating your model, read through the included instruction sheet. Then choose a theme and make a plan. Do you want to make a replica of Groot from Marvel's *Guardians of the Galaxy*, or something completely different? The choice is yours! Here are some sample projects to get those creative juices flowing.

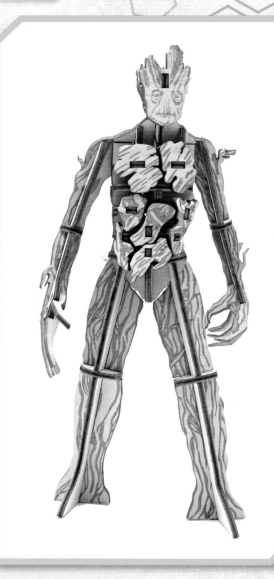

I AM GROOT

WHAT YOU NEED:
- Light brown, dark brown, white, black, green, and orange-yellow colored pencils

WHAT YOU MIGHT WANT:
- More shades of brown colored pencils
- Brown paint

TIP: If you want to use colored pencils, color the pieces before you build. For paints, you will want to build the model before painting.

STEPS

1 Start with the face, piece 23.
Color the eyes white.

2 Add black dots on top of the white for pupils.

3 Fill in the area around the eyes with a dark brown colored pencil.

4 Color the rest of the face light brown.

5 Add some subtle hints of orange-yellow to the pieces.

6 Add a small bit of green towards the top of the head.

7 To blend this all together, add a light layer of light brown.

8 Color the rest of the pieces light brown.

9 Once you've finished coloring, assemble the model.

10 If you'd like, paint the edges of the pieces once you have assembled the model.

GO A STEP FURTHER

1 Color the engravings dark brown.

2 Add another layer of light brown to blend.

3 Add green and orange-yellow to each of the pieces, as you like.

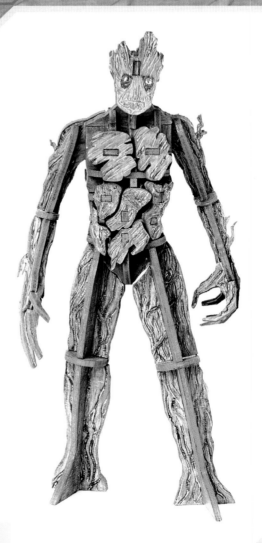

TIP: The key to coloring Groot is blending the colored pencils. Layer the colors until you achieve the effect you like.

WE ARE GROOT

As *Dark Aster* crashed to Xandar, the guardians were left plummeting towards the ground. Groot, however, grew his branches and leaves around his fellow guardians—cushioning them for the fall and saving their lives. While it's more difficult to change the shape of an IncrediBuilds model, this project allows for an ode to Groot's heroism.

WHAT YOU NEED:

- Medium paintbrush
- Very small paintbrush
- White, black, light brown, dark brown, light green, dark green, and yellow paint

WHAT YOU MIGHT WANT:

- Glitter glue
- Toothpick

STEPS

1 | Build the model completely before you start to paint.

2 | Paint the eyes white.

3 | Add black dots for the pupils of the eyes.

4 | Before adding any more detail, paint the rest of the model light brown. Let dry.

5 | Using a very small paintbrush or a toothpick, paint the area around the eyes dark brown.

6 | Add dark brown paint to the engraving marks on the face.

7 | Trace the rest of the engravings on the model using the same dark brown paint.

8 | Take dark green paint and paint vines and leaves over the entire model.

9 | Go back over the dark green paint with light green paint, leaving some of the dark green paint showing around the edges of the leaves and vines.

10 | Use a toothpick to make dots of yellow on the model for the glow spores.

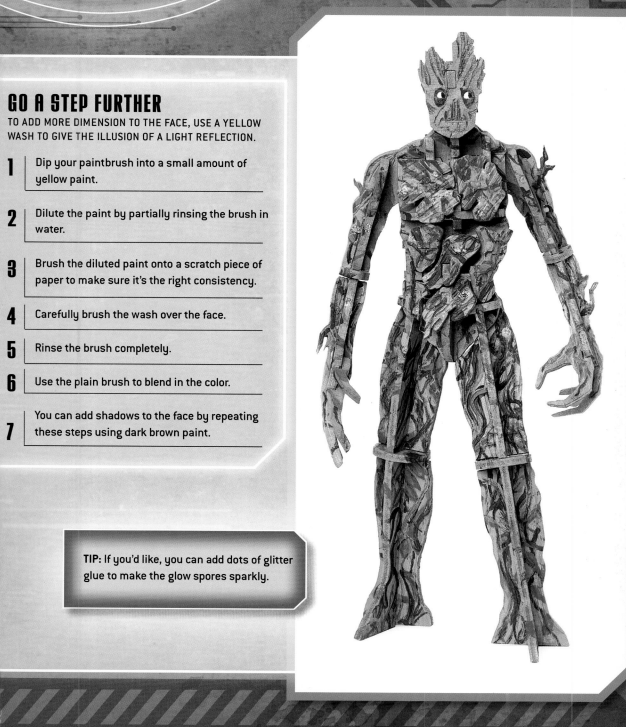

GO A STEP FURTHER

TO ADD MORE DIMENSION TO THE FACE, USE A YELLOW
WASH TO GIVE THE ILLUSION OF A LIGHT REFLECTION.

1 Dip your paintbrush into a small amount of
yellow paint.

2 Dilute the paint by partially rinsing the brush in
water.

3 Brush the diluted paint onto a scratch piece of
paper to make sure it's the right consistency.

4 Carefully brush the wash over the face.

5 Rinse the brush completely.

6 Use the plain brush to blend in the color.

7 You can add shadows to the face by repeating
these steps using dark brown paint.

TIP: If you'd like, you can add dots of glitter
glue to make the glow spores sparkly.

INSIGHT EDITIONS

A Division of Insight Editions, LP
PO Box 3088
San Rafael, CA 94912
www.insighteditions.com

 Find us on Facebook: www.facebook.com/InsightEditions
Follow us on Twitter: @insighteditions

© 2017 MARVEL

Library of Congress Cataloging-in-Publication Data available.

ISBN:978-1-68298-070-5

Publisher: Raoul Goff
Acquisitions Manager: Robbie Schmidt
Art Director: Chrissy Kwasnik
Designer: Ashley Quackenbush
Executive Editor: Vanessa Lopez
Associate Editor: Katie DeSandro
Production Editor: Elaine Ou
Production Coordinator: Sam Taylor
Craft and Instruction Development: Rebekah Piatte
Model Design: HeJian Zhu, Team Green

 REPLANTED PAPER

Insight Editions, in association with Roots of Peace, will plant two trees for each tree used in the manufacturing
of this book. Roots of Peace is an internationally renowned humanitarian organization dedicated to eradicating
land mines worldwide and converting war-torn lands into productive farms and wildlife habitats. Roots of Peace
will plant two million fruit and nut trees in Afghanistan and provide farmers there with the skills and support
necessary for sustainable land use.

Manufactured in China by Insight Editions

10 9 8 7 6 5 4 3 2 1